HONEY

The Dog Who Saved Abe Lincoln

Written by **Shari Swanson**

Illustrated by **Chuck Groenink**

KATHERINE TEGEN BOOKS
An Imprint of HarperCollins Publishers

Katherine Tegen Books is an imprint of HarperCollins Publishers.

Honey, the Dog Who Saved Abe Lincoln

Text copyright © 2020 by Shari Swanson

Illustrations copyright © 2020 by Chuck Groenink

Library of Congress Control Number: 2019021370

ISBN 978-0-06-269901-5

The artist used Photoshop to create the digital illustrations for this book.

Typography by Rachel Zegar

23 24 25   RRDA   10 9 8 7 6 5 4 3 2

❖

First trade paperback edition, 2021

For Lily and Ella
—S.S.

Young Abraham Lincoln was kneeling deep in the woods when three shrill blasts of a whistle cut through the quiet. His corn was ready at the mill, and he was late.

Watching a frog limp away into the brush, Abe smiled.

It wasn't every day he was able to rescue a frog right out of a snake's mouth.

Abe hurried back to where Mr. John Hodgen, the miller, was waiting. "Now, Abe, what took you so long this time?" Mr. John asked.

"I just can't move along fast like some boys, Mr. John, because I see so many little foolish things that make me stop. I can't help it to save my life."

Mr. John patted the boy's head and handed him a sack of ground corn. "Now get on your way, Abe. You'd best be home before dark."

Abe heaved the bag onto his shoulder and set off on the long path that wound its way like a rusty snake through the Knob Creek hills to the Lincolns' log cabin.

Abe had only a mile or so left to go when
something caught his attention. He froze.
What was rustling in the bushes?

Beneath some brambles at the base of a cliff, Abe found a dog whimpering softly.

The dog's front leg was broken.

"Did you fall, boy?" Abe asked. The dog looked up into Abe's eyes, wagging his tail.

Abe patted the gentle dog's head and looked around for something to use to set the leg.

He was only seven years old, but Abe had spent his whole life on a Kentucky farm and knew how to tend to animals.

He pared two sticks smooth with his pocketknife to
make a splint. Then he peeled the soft bark off a pawpaw
bush to wrap around the sticks.

Finally, he tied it all around the dog's leg with some
rawhide from his belt.

By the time Abe was through, the sun was slanting low through the trees. Abe hefted the bag of ground corn back onto his shoulder and called to the dog. The dog struggled up and limped along after Abe on his three good legs.

Abe was going to be late. That wasn't unusual. But this time he would have a dog to explain.

Abe's father was asleep by the fire when Abe got home, but his mother was waiting up. "Oh, Abraham, where have you been off to this time? Didn't you know I would be worried?"

"I found a real honey of a dog. His leg is broken," Abe whispered.

"Please let me keep him."
Abe looked up at his mother.
"He'll do lots of good things for me,"
he told her. "You just watch and see."

Nancy could never say no to her beloved boy, so the dog stayed.
Abe snuck Honey scraps of food, and soon the dog was able to walk.

Honey's leg looked like a curve
in the road, but that didn't stop him
from trotting along after Abe on
their adventures.

Everywhere Abraham went, Honey went.

One day, Abe showed up late to drop off
his grain at the mill. Mr. John shook his head.
    "Why do you fool your time away?" he
asked Abe. "You have seen these hills and hollows
hundreds of times. I can't understand what you find
to keep you so long on the road."

"Well, Mr. John," Abe answered, "Honey got a possum in a hollow stump, and I couldn't get him to leave it, and I couldn't leave Honey."

Abe wandered off a bit to wait his turn. He took out a soapstone pencil to practice writing his letters on a bit of bark. But soon, the woods were calling, and Abe got the itch to answer.

Before long, he and Honey found themselves at
the mouth of a cave. Deep, twisting caverns traveled for
hundreds of miles under Kentucky. A boy and his dog could
get lost in caverns like these. And, sure enough, disaster struck.
Abe got jammed between two boulders and couldn't move.

Try as he might, pulling
himself this way, that way, and
back again, he was hopelessly stuck,
and night was beginning to fall.
Honey whimpered and pawed at the
ground. Abe couldn't move. Honey
normally never left Abe, but this time
he headed alone back into the darkening
woods. Honey would need to get help.

Back at the mill, the entire town had gathered in the night to search for Abe. Mr. John had been blowing and blowing on his whistle, but Abe hadn't come.

Nancy Lincoln asked Mr. John, "Have you seen the dog, Mr. Hodgen?
Was Honey with Abraham when he came to the mill?"

"Yes, the dog was with him," answered Mr. John.

Abe's mother was grateful for Honey. It comforted her to know Abe
had him for protection. She waited anxiously at the edge of the dark forest,
hoping her boy would come home.

Then she heard something rustling in the bushes.

"Here's Honey! Here's Honey!" she called.
Suddenly, Honey emerged from the bushes, barking
and whining at Nancy's feet.

The dog looked up into the faces of one after another until he got to
Mr. John. Then Honey jumped up on Mr. John and barked in his face.
"Grab your torches," called Mr. John. "We'll follow where the dog leads."

Yelping and panting, Honey headed back through the woods.

The townsfolk followed behind him, their torches parting the night.

When they got to the cave entrance, Honey stopped.
The townsfolk were afraid. Many a silent prayer went
up for the boy's safety.

Mr. John blew three times on his cane-pole whistle.

"Here I am," called Abe, his voice echoing from deep within the cavern. "But I'm fastened."

Mr. John carefully made his way into the damp, narrow tunnel. He found Abraham tightly wedged but had no room to swing a sledge to break the rocks.

Mr. John could only tug Abe out, even though it meant leaving some of the boy's hide behind.

Once Abe was back up into the night air, Nancy rushed to hold her beloved son and his precious dog.

Abraham was surprised at the crowd. He smiled at his mother. "I knew Honey would do great things for me," he said. "Now he has paid me back for mending his broken leg."

The next day, and for many more days after that, Abe and Honey were back at their adventures, bumping and scrambling their way along the banks of Knob Creek. A boy and his loyal dog, Honey.

Timeline of Abraham Lincoln and His Animal Encounters

The Kentucky Years
1809–1816

February 12, 1809

✷ Abraham Lincoln is born during a fierce winter storm at the Sinking Spring Farm in Kentucky, where he lives with his parents, Thomas and Nancy, and big sister, Sarah.

Spring 1811

✷ The Lincoln family moves a few miles away to a farm in Knob Creek, Kentucky.

1814

✷ Abe's father buys him a toy wagon at auction for eight and a half cents.

1815–1816

✷ Young Abe has many chores on the family farm. He fetches water, feeds the animals, plants crops, fishes, chops wood, cleans ashes from the fireplace, picks berries, and walks to Hodgen's Mill to have corn ground into cornmeal.

✷ The miller, Mr. John, and the miller's mother, Missus Sarah, help teach Abe how to read.

✷ Abe finds an injured dog, names him Honey, and nurses him back to health.

✷ Honey saves Abe and his friend Austin from a wildcat.

✷ Honey saves Abe from being trapped in a cavern.

✷ Abe spends his free time studying various animals in the forest.

The Indiana Years
1816–1830

December 1816

✷ Abe moves with his family and Honey to a farm near Little Pigeon Creek, Indiana, shortly after Indiana enters the country as a free (nonslave) state.

February 1817

✷ Abe shoots a turkey and vows never to kill large game again.

October 5, 1818

✷ Nancy Lincoln dies from "milk sickness," first telling her children to be good and kind to their father, each other, and the world.

1819

✷ Abe's father remarries. Sarah Lincoln, her three children, and their pet cat move in.

✷ Abe lectures to the neighboring children about the wickedness of cruelty to animals. He says, "Even an ant values its life."

The Illinois Years
1830–1860

* Abe's dog, possibly Honey, falls behind as the Lincolns and three other families are fording an icy stream in their ox-driven wagons. Abe takes off his shoes and wades, waist deep, across the partly frozen stream to carry his dog to safety.

* Abe risks his new good suit to put baby birds blown to the ground safely back in their nest and, a different time, to rescue a pig floundering in the mud.

November 4, 1842

* Abe marries Mary Todd. They have four sons together: Robert Todd (1843–1926), Edward Baker (1846–1850), William Wallace (1850–1862), and Thomas "Tad" (1853–1871).

January 17, 1851

* Abe's father, Thomas, dies.

The Washington, D.C., Years
1860–1865

1861

* After Abe is elected president, the Lincolns move to Washington, D.C. Their dog Fido sits for a photographer, becoming the first presidential pet photographed.

* The Lincoln White House is full of animals, including goats Nanny and Nanko. The Lincolns' son Tad harnesses Nanko to a chair and "rides" triumphantly through an elegant reception while the ladies in attendance hold their hoop skirts out of the way.

* The Civil War begins.

1863

* President Lincoln issues the Emancipation Proclamation on January 1, freeing all slaves in rebel states.

* Lincoln delivers the Gettysburg Address on November 19.

* Yielding to Tad's pleas, Lincoln "pardons" the turkey intended for Christmas dinner.

1865

* Abe visits the headquarters of General Grant on the battlefield and notices three motherless kittens. He says, "I hope you will see that these poor motherless waifs are given plenty of milk and treated kindly."

* Shortly after the end of the Civil War and his election to a second term, on April 15, Lincoln is assassinated. His body, and that of his deceased son Willy, are taken back to Springfield, Illinois, for burial. Fido comforts the mourners, and their horse Old Bob, dressed in a gray blanket with silver tassels, follows, riderless, immediately behind the hearse in the funeral procession.

Author's Note

Before he was president of the United States, Abraham Lincoln was a young boy running barefoot through the hills and hollows of Knob Creek, Kentucky. He was born during a fierce winter storm on February 12, 1809, and spent the first years of his life in a one-room log cabin with just one tiny window peeking out onto the wild, untamed world.

The events of this story are true as remembered by Abe's childhood best friend, Austin Gollaher. Back then, before people learned to read and write, they passed on stories orally. Austin enjoyed telling boys and girls the stories about his childhood adventures with Abraham Lincoln. One Kentucky child, J. Rogers Gore, grew up to be a journalist who wrote the stories down in a book, *The Boyhood of Abraham Lincoln: From the Spoken Narratives of Austin Gollaher.* For the most part, the incidents and quotations are recounted here exactly as Austin remembered them—or heard tell of them from Abe or other people in town. Austin told Mr. Gore these stories many decades after they happened, so they might not have been relayed perfectly, but undoubtedly the essence of Abe's friendship with Honey is true.

Austin fondly remembered his adventures with Abe and Honey. He told of the time Honey saved them from a wildcat. And of the time when a scraggly stranger with a long scar curving from his eye to his mouth came into town and claimed that Honey was his dog, Whistle. And his saddest story, when he watched the Lincolns leave for Indiana. The two boys hugged their goodbyes, then Abe broke away to lead the family cow across the stream, Honey following behind.

Honey wasn't the only animal Abe saved when he lived in Kentucky. He had a tame crow that he and Austin tried to teach to talk, a goat they tried to teach to pull a cart, and a tame racoon that Honey would herd back into the yard if it strayed. Abe also released many animals from traps set by his father in the woods, much to his father's dismay.

When he became president, Abraham Lincoln filled the White House with animals, including a little goat that pulled his son Tad through the halls in a cart.

Today you can visit a replica of Abe's childhood cabin nestled next to Knob Creek, among the hills and hollows of Hodgenville, Kentucky, where Abe and Honey once roamed free.